MORTIMER WALKER'S GUIDE

CONTENTS

INTRODUCTION

It is hard to imagine any better place to walk than in the Marches, the borderland country of England and Wales. This is where gentle pastures give way to high hills and mountains. Here you will find The Mortimer Trail, a 30 mile walking route from Ludlow to Kington which follows a succession of ridges in a north east to south-westerly direction. It is so called because this was the very heartland of the Mortimer family, holders of the most powerful of the Norman Earldoms.

Each mile of this Trail holds promise. It passes through forests where tracts of broadleaved woodland give way to coniferous stands. Here you will find fallow deer grazing in the cover of Mortimer Forest or Shobdon Hill Wood. The route descends from the high ridges to the water's edge of the Teme, Lugg and Arrow rivers where kingfisher and heron can be seen. Climbs are constantly rewarded by views of the Forest of Radnor, the Black Mountains, Clee Hills and, of course, the majestic Malvern Hills. Pause awhile to admire the worn lines of ancient hillforts and medieval castles holding fast the secrets of previous ages, now the haunt of buzzard and raven.

There are, without doubt, countless aspects to savour at the end of a day's walking. But there's nothing quite so inspiring as watching the reddened sun fall behind Cole Hill on a late winter afternoon.

It is a route to be cherished for there are few such areas so rich in natural history and human heritage. Pass through quietly and you will see and hear wildlife close at hand and preserve the very appeal which makes the area rather special to the country goer.

For the most part The Mortimer Trail is a high level route away from settlements which are to be found in the gaps and river valleys below. While the hills are rarely over 1,000 feet, you will find climbs which are strenuous in places such as at High Vinnals, Shobdon Hill Wood and Byton.

There are, however, five Loop Walks - Yarpole, Wigmore, Lingen, Shobdon and Titley, which allow you to descend from the ridges to seek refreshment and accommodation or public transport back to a starting point. For example, it is possible to walk out of Ludlow on the main Trail to Croft Ambrey and then head north on the Loop to Wigmore, eventually returning by bus. The Loops also make for splendid circular half day and day walks.

THE LANDSCAPE

The north west corner of Herefordshire and south Shropshire are characterised by a series of rock formations which give rise to a number of limestone edges. These dip to valleys where softer shales have been eroded, most probably during post glacial times. These rocks were classified in the last century by the famous geologist, Sir Roderick Murcheson, as part of the Silurian System which were formed some 400 million years ago. There is a fascinating geological trail at Mortimer Forest, known as the Mortimer Forest Geology Trail, which explores and explains the geology and fossil bearing strata of the area.

Most of the upland areas are covered with woodlands many of which are managed by Forest Enterprise. On The Mortimer Trail, tree cover along several sections has been thinned to encourage a variety of wildlife and to offer improved views. Ash, oak, beech and lime are common broadleaves with birch, hazel and thorn in hedgerows on adjacent farmland. The coniferous blocks are mainly larch, Douglas Fir and Norway spruce although others are grown such as the Scots and Corsican pine.

The Mortimer Trail crosses three beautiful river valleys - the Teme, Lugg and Arrow and their tributaries. The Arrow, which is approached by the Trail near Kington, flows into the Lugg below Leominster. The Lugg in turn joins the River Wye at Mordiford. The Teme flows through to the River Severn near Worcester.

All three rise in the mountains of Powys although the Arrow soon reaches Herefordshire. They are known to be virtually free of pollution and therefore attract wildlife. Accordingly, the River Lugg has been designated as a 'Site of Special Scientific Interest' by English Nature, a designation which affords special conservation status. The rivers support a variety of fish including brown trout and salmon, whilst an otter population has returned to colonise them once more.

For the most part the Mortimer Trail passes through farmland which is primarily permanent pasture used to fatten stock or rear sheep for sale at local markets. There is very little arable farming except on the lower slopes towards Shobdon and Titley. Here cereals, potatoes and fruit crops are grown in addition to intensive farming of poultry. There are few cider apple orchards in this part of Herefordshire but you will see by some farms small traditional orchards with standard size trees. These have been planted primarily for domestic use.

The Landscape - continued...

One significant feature along the Trail is the number of commons. Some, such as Whitcliffe and Bircher, are managed by commoners or graziers whilst others, Byton and Yatton for example, are privately owned. They are used mainly for grazing sheep but local people also enjoy the amenity of these open spaces near to their homes.

WILDLIFE

The wildlife of the area is rich and varied. There are hundreds of species of wild flowers to observe from the shade loving primrose, anemone and the bluebell in spring to the rich profusion of meadow flowers swaying in the summer breeze, flowers such as buttercup, vetch, milkwort and daisy. There are orchids in certain locations too. By the path you'll find an ever changing range of plant life - hemp nettle, ground elder, charlock and poppies, bramble and scented rose, bracken and gorse. These varied habitats attract butterflies, two of which enjoy the woodland and are quite unexpected, the comma and silver-washed fritillary.

The rich cover of woodland is home to many birds including magpie, jay and woodpecker. The woods also attract a number of unusual species such as siskin, crossbills and goldcrests, as well as summer visitors such as warblers and flycatchers who live off the rich insect life of the forest. Both in the woodland and above the upland commons you are likely to see birds of prey such as the kestrel, sparrow-hawk and buzzard, and on occasion rarer species. They can sometimes be seen perched on vantage points or circling in the sky in a search of mice and voles on the hillsides below.

Throughout the walk you are likely to encounter rabbit, hare and fox and the woodland areas also attract polecats. In the quieter areas of the woods you will almost certainly come across fallow, roe and muntjac deer or at least see their droppings on or near the path. You may also come across badger sets but please do not disturb them.

ANCIENT CAMPS
AND ROMAN ROADS

O
ne of the joys of the Trail is the visual evidence of past human activity, from the earliest recorded history of hunter-gatherer tribes who lived almost entirely on the high ground to the landscaped parklands set out by our Georgian and Victorian forefathers.

A similar high level route would have certainly been known to ancient tribal groups. Evidence of early settlements can be seen at Croft Ambrey (390BC) and Wapley where there are Iron Age hillforts. Burial cists and mounds have also been found in the area through which The Mortimer Trail passes, in the Lugg Valley and near Kington, for example.

To the Romans, the Marches could best be described as a frontierland as they sought to gain a powerful grip over warring tribal groups such as the Silures. The Mortimer Trail descends to the Lugg Gap (a gorge eroded in post-glacial times) at Aymestrey to cross a Roman road between the garrison towns of Kenchester (Magnis), near Hereford and Leintwardine (Branogenium).

It appears that there was endless warfare in this border region throughout the Dark Ages. Offa's Dyke is a reminder of these times, built by the *bretwalda* (overlord) 'King Offa', to retain economic and political stability against the Welsh. The warfare continued through the medieval period and the entire borderland is dotted with the ruins and earthworks of Norman strongholds. Further strife occurred up to and during the English Civil War of the 1640s, although between uprisings life would have continued its peaceful pastoral pace.

A milestone near Mortimer's Cross

THE MORTIMERS

From these earlier times remain a network of ways and tracks, early village sites and the field systems around them. Much of what remains, however, can be traced back to medieval times when castle and church, farmstead and mill were established according to the rules of the Norman feudal system. Of the medieval Marcher Earls, there were none more powerful than the Mortimers whose seat of power was at Wigmore Castle.

Their story is one of intrigue and alliance between King and barons, and with the Welsh princes too. The Mortimers' degree of involvement in the affairs of state was significant. The first to reside at Wigmore was Ralph de Mortimer. It was given to him as a reward for his support at a time when the FitzOsbern family had lost favour in these parts. A succession of Mortimers ruled hereabouts for well over three centuries, some of whom are more notable than others.

In 1246, the sixth Lord of Wigmore, Roger Mortimer, continued the seemingly endless battle against the revered Welsh prince Llewelyn ap Gruffyd, a most bloody and destructive combat. Roger also supported Henry III against an uprising led by Simon de Montfort, which brought great reward for the Mortimers after the King quelled the insurrection at the Battle of Evesham and Roger sent home the head of de Montfort as a trophy for his wife.

In the early decades of the 14th century, however, the Mortimers plotted against the then monarch, Edward II. Roger Mortimer was imprisoned in The Tower of London but escaped to France to join his lover, Edward's unfaithful Queen Isabella, and her son Prince Edward. From there they led an invasion of England, deposed Edward II and eventually had him murdered in Berkeley Castle. The young prince became Edward III and on reaching maturity decided that Roger was something of a threat. He was hung, drawn and quartered at Tyburn.

Almost a century later, Edmund Mortimer was declared the rightful heir to the throne in 1415 at the age of 14 but he was not to achieve this. Despite his allegiance he was banished to Ireland by Henry VI. There he died at the age of 24 and without a successor. However, descendants of the Mortimers did come to power in the 15th century.

Edmund's great nephew became the Yorkist King Edward IV after the defeat of Lancastrian troops at the Battle of Mortimer's Cross in 1461.

Edward is chronicled as one of the more progressive kings of the time but the direct Mortimer line was cut by the death of Richard III at the Battle of Bosworth Field (1485) although through marriage ties Mortimer blood ran in the veins of the Tudor dynasty.

Their importance in these times were unmistakable. Wigmore and Ludlow castles witnessed the ascendancy of the Mortimer Earls and so they shaped the local communities which grew up under the manorial system.

How to Use The Guide

In this Guide the main Mortimer Trail route has been divided into 4 sections of between 5 and 11 miles.

Within each section there are walking instructions which are cross referenced by number to the adjacent map.

The distance and nature of the Trail is indicated as are other useful details.

When walking please always remember to...

- *Tell someone where you are going.*

- *Wear appropriate clothing and boots. The paths often get muddy after rain and there are climbs and descents which necessitate sturdy footwear.*

- *Carry adequate clothing in case the weather turns inclement. A small knapsack for a jumper, waterproofs and a snack is ideal.*

- *Carry a first aid kit and if walking in winter when snow, rain or mist is likely take a compass, torch and whistle in case you get into difficulties along the more remote sections.*

- *Follow the Country Code.*

- *Keep all dogs on a lead.*

- *Please retain the peace and quiet of the route and be sensitive to local communities and wildlife.*

Map Information and Waymarks

The Mortimer Trail is covered by two Ordnance Survey 'Landranger' maps (1:50,000), Sheet *137 Ludlow & Wenlock Edge* and *148 Presteigne and Hay-on-Wye*.

For more detailed mapping consult the Ordnance Survey 'Pathfinder' sheets (1:25,000)
951 Ludlow
972 Tenbury Wells
971 Presteigne
993 Kington

The whole of the route is 'waymarked' with special waymark sign-posts. These are easily recognisable by their Mortimer Trail logo discs. Additional discs on waymark posts indicate the type of path, eg public footpath, permissive path, bridleway etc. The Loop Walks (Circular Walks) are also waymarked.

The full route of the Mortimer Trail is shown on the back cover. This diagram shows how the sketch maps in this Guide piece together.

Fitting waymark discs to a waymark post

Ludlow

A

Orleton Common

Byton   **C**   **B**

Aymestrey

D

The Mortimer Trail logo

Titley

E

Map A Ludlow to Orleton Common - page 15
Map B Orleton Common to Aymestrey - page 19
Map C Aymestrey to Byton - page 23
Map D Byton to Titley - page 25
Map E Titley to Kington - page 29

Kington

LUDLOW TO ORLETON COMMON

Distance: 8 miles (13km)

Terrain

There are several climbs up to Mortimer Forest and High Vinnals (over 1200 feet). Walking is mainly on forest tracks through to Hanway Common and then along a bridleway to The Goggin. The last section is road walking but these lanes are quiet.

Access

Ludlow is well served by trains from Manchester and the North West, Shrewsbury, Hereford and Cardiff. Buses from Birmingham and Hereford stop in Corve Street. The Mortimer Trail is waymarked from both the station and bus stops to Ludlow Castle.

There are several car parks in Ludlow.

Cut Off Points

Richard's Castle. From Hanway Common it is possible to walk down to The Castle Inn from where there is a daily bus to Ludlow. 1.5 miles (2.5km)

Orleton Common. From Orleton Common it is possible to walk down to The Maidenhead pub from where there is a daily bus to Ludlow. 1 mile (1.6km)

Refreshment

There are several cafes and pubs in Ludlow but nothing on this section of the Trail unless you divert to Richard's Castle for the Castle Inn, or Orleton where you will find The Maidenhead Inn, The Boot Inn and a village stores.

Ludlow Castle

Ludlow to Orleton Common - continued...

PLACES OF INTEREST

Ludlow

Ludlow has been described as one of the finest country towns in England. Its compact medieval town layout makes it so walkable and there are half timbered Tudor buildings and Georgian town houses throughout. It is also refreshing to see many small shops in the high streets and stalls are set out in Castle Square on market day.

The Castle stands at the top of the Square, a formidable fortification high above the Rivers Teme and Corve. It dates originally from the 11th century but there are written records from 1138. It was held by the de Lacy family but they were very often away in Ireland. In the 13th century it passed to the de Genevilles then through marriage to the Mortimers in the early 14th century.

During the English Civil War Ludlow Castle was held by the Royalists and suffered badly until surrendered to the Parliamentarians. From this time it fell into decline until 1811 when the Castle passed into the hands of the Earls of Powis who still administer it to this day. It is open to the public and is home to the celebrated Ludlow Festival every summer.

Mortimer Forest

This is the name used by Forest Enterprise to describe the various woodlands it manages throughout the central Marches but it is also used to describe the main forest of over 1,000 hectares near to Ludlow. There are several woodland trails and numerous events organised throughout the year reflecting Forest Enterprise's approach to recreational use of their land. See also their waymarked 'Geological Trail'.

Mortimer Forest

Whitcliffe, Climbing Jack and Hanway Commons

The Mortimer Trail runs through a number of commons. The first is Whitcliffe which offers great views of Ludlow and is much loved by the people of the town.

Climbing Jack is well known as a place where deer can be seen grazing its quieter corners. The name is derived from an old spelling of a plot known as Climbers Oak or in those days Climbers Ake and has been altered over the years.

Hanway is a rich grazing pasture with splendid views and local folklore has it that 'Colonel', the Grand National winner of 1886, was trained on these slopes.

Richard's Castle

From Hanway it is possible to drop down to the scant ruins of Richard's Castle, one of the earliest Norman castles in Herefordshire built by Richard FitzOsbern, hence the name. Standing near to the earthworks is a beautiful Norman church with a detached tower dating from the 14th century. It is no longer the parish church but is open to the public.

Orleton and Orleton Common

Orleton Common is a hamlet on the spring line beneath Woodcroft and Patrick's hills. One mile away lies Orleton, a much larger village where you will find a number of half-timbered dwellings including Orleton Court. Adam of Orleton was born here and as the then Bishop of Hereford he plotted the death of Edward II with Roger de Mortimer.

ROUTE DETAILS
LUDLOW - ORLETON COMMON

● *There is a waymarked Mortimer Trail link from Ludlow Railway Station to Ludlow Castle. Cross Station Drive, go right and proceed to Corve St. Turn left to walk up to the Bull Ring, passing bus stops and also the half timbered Feathers Hotel. Bear right into King Street and continue ahead to Castle Square via High Street (the Tourist Information Centre is on the left).*

1 Facing the entrance to Ludlow Castle turn right to walk beneath the castle walls to the west facing edge overlooking the flowing waters of the River Teme. The path forks and you take the lower route down to the Linney. Go left along the road and at the junction turn right to cross Dinham Bridge.

2 At the far side the Mortimer Trail leaves the road to climb steps up to Whitcliffe Common. Go right at the top and follow the path around as it bends left, dips to a cross track and continues to a road. Go right down to a bend.
Caution:
Cliff Edges are subject to collapse. Please heed warning signs and keep to footpath.

3 Cross with care into the No Through Road but within a few paces go left. The path forks and you choose the lower one again. This climbs steadily up through Mortimer Forest to a junction beneath a car parking area. Go left up to the lay-by and cross over the Wigmore Road.

4 Climb up the wide forestry track to pass by the Forest Enterprise Offices. The track bears right and then sweeps left. It descends towards the Mary Knoll Valley. Follow it as it bends sharply right and dips to another sharp bend. Here you continue ahead along a narrow path which leads down to a small brook.

5 Once over go left but then within a few paces bear right up a path which climbs the hillside. This reaches a cross roads at the top where you turn right to rise more gradually by a sunken track. Cross the main forestry track and continue along a track which runs through Climbing Jack Common.

6 As the main track bends left keep ahead to enter woodland again and still rising. You soon reach a fork. Keep left here to climb up to High Vinnals, 370 metres high (1,200 feet), then descend to a junction of forestry tracks. Go left and almost immediately right.

7 Follow the well used green track through to a gate. Go through it to Hanway Common. Keep company with the hedge on the right. You reach a metalled road leading to Vallets Farm on the right.

● *This is a link down the road to Richard's Castle, The Castle Inn and bus stops (link not waymarked).*

8 Continue along the hedge on your right but as it bears right head slightly left to join another hedge. Keep ahead as the common tapers to a gate. Go through it and walk down the bridleway to a metalled road at The Goggin.

9 Turn left and then at the next junction right. Climb up to the bluff and then drop to another junction. Go left and follow Stockin Lane along its entire length to the edge of Orleton Common. Go right down the hillside, taking care here as there is more traffic. At the junction turn right and you soon reach a junction with Waterloo Lane to your right.

● *This is the link route to Orleton where there is a shop, two pubs The Maidenhead and the Boot Inn and bus stops. (Keep left down Waterloo Lane to reach Orleton via Green Lane).*

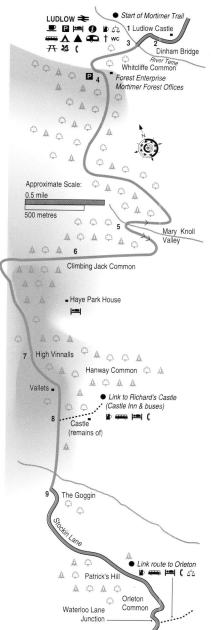

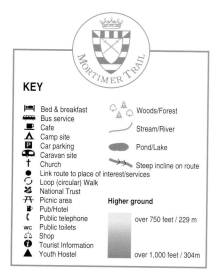

KEY

🛏	Bed & breakfast	🌲 Woods/Forest	
🚌	Bus service		
☕	Cafe	Stream/River	
⛺	Camp site		
🅿	Car parking	Pond/Lake	
🚐	Caravan site		
†	Church	Steep incline on route	
●	Link route to place of interest/services		
↻	Loop (circular) Walk	**Higher ground**	
National Trust		
🌲	Picnic area		
🍺	Pub/Hotel	over 750 feet / 229 m	
(	Public telephone		
wc	Public toilets		
Shop		
❶	Tourist Information		
▲	Youth Hostel	over 1,000 feet / 304m	

Map labels:
LUDLOW — Start of Mortimer Trail — 1 Ludlow Castle — 2 Dinham Bridge — River Teme — 3 — Whitcliffe Common — Forest Enterprise Mortimer Forest Offices — 4 — Mary Knoll Valley — 5 — 6 — Climbing Jack Common — Haye Park House — High Vinnalls — 7 — Hanway Common — Vallets — Link to Richard's Castle (Castle Inn & buses) — 8 — Castle (remains of) — 9 The Goggin — Stockin Lane — Link route to Orleton — Patrick's Hill — Orleton Common — Waterloo Lane Junction

Approximate Scale:
0.5 mile
500 metres

ORLETON COMMON TO AYMESTREY

Distance: 5 miles (8km)

Terrain

The route rises through farmland up to Bircher Common, 280 metres (918 feet) and then is relatively level through to Croft Wood and Croft Ambrey, 300 metres (984 feet).

Access

There is a daily bus service 292 to/from Ludlow to the Maidenhead pub in Orleton which is 1 mile from the route. There is no suitable parking in this area for cars.

Cut-Off Points

Croft Castle and Aymestrey.

Refreshment

Riverside Inn and shop in Aymestrey.

Church Tower at Croft Castle

PLACES OF INTEREST

Bircher, Leinthall and Yatton Commons

Bircher is the largest of the commons on the route and is crowned by Oaker Coppice, a mixed woodland which appears to have been fenced at one time. At the southern edges there are a number of cottages and houses, which like Orleton Common, have settled along the spring line of wells and small streams. Commoners still graze their animals here, including pigs, goats and geese!

Leinthall and Yatton commons are clothed in broadleaved woodland. The climb up from Yatton is ferocious but the views exquisite.

Croft Castle

The stone castle at Croft dates originally from the 14 and 15th centuries. It was built on the site of previous fortified structures for the Croft Family who have lived here since the time of Edward the Confessor with a break of 170 years from 1750. The house contains many different styles of interior design mainly from the 18th century including an impressive grand staircase as well as a collection of Gothic furniture. In the parkland nearby stands a serene little church. Inside, you will find the magnificent tombs of Sir Richard Croft and his wife dating from the early 16th century. The entire Estate is managed by the National Trust and is open to the public.

Croft Ambrey

Croft Ambrey stands at nearly 1,000 feet and is one of the best examples of an Iron Age hillfort. It is a large, multi-enclosure site which dates from about 390 BC. It's now in the care of the National Trust; take care not to damage the ramparts or mounds therein.

Lucton

From Lucton Common it is possible to walk half a mile down to Lucton village and school founded in 1708 by a London merchant. Near to Lucton Church and New House Farm is a field path to Mortimer's Cross, by far the best route from The Mortimer Trail to the Mortimer's Cross Inn as you avoid the traffic on the B4362.

Mortimer's Cross

The bloody battle of 1461 took place near to the existing crossroads but the only monument to remind us of this turning point in history is outside the Monument Inn at Kingsland. It was a bitterly cold Candlemas Day in February when Edward (of Mortimer descent) led Yorkist troops to defeat the Lancastrians and hence secured the throne for himself as Edward IV. The Mortimer's Cross Inn and a milestone reflect coaching days of a later era. There's also a water mill by the Lugg which is open to the public, although opening times are limited. The mill also houses a battlefield museum.

Aymestrey

At a bridging point of the River Lugg on what was a Roman road (now the A4110 here) lies the village of Aymestrey. The Riverside Inn and parish church with surrounding orchards make a very pleasant setting. One of the bells in the church used to be rung each evening to guide bewitched travellers making their way through Pokeshouse (derivation Puck) Wood. A sum of money was set aside by a poor unfortunate soul who had spent a night lost and tormented in these woods but that has long since been exhausted! On the way into Aymestrey you pass by the handsome Georgian building, Yatton Court. On the route out to Ballsgate Common you pass by Aymestrey Mill which produced flour until the 1960s.

ROUTE DETAILS -
ORLETON COMMON TO AYMESTREY

10   At the junction with Waterloo Lane keep left but at the next junction, which is no more than 100 metres on, turn right as signposted. The track climbs past a dwelling and continues to pass Spout House. Here, you continue ahead up a narrow path which lies to the left of outbuildings.

11   At the road, go right. At the corner T junction keep left and rise up to pass two houses. Now look for a stile and signpost on the right leading into a field.

12   Climb the bank as close as you can to an old track which is covered by scrub. The views across to the Malvern Hills are superb. Proceed through three fields, for the most part following a tractor track, and keeping near to the hedge on your right. You soon reach Lodge Farm. The path runs through the upper farmyard to the right of the farmhouse and a brick outbuilding. After this take care not to branch right. Keep ahead along a green track which runs through bracken, still keeping company with the hedge on your right.

13   The path reaches the top right hand corner of the field. Go left here to a cross a stile next to a barred gate which leads to Bircher Common. Walk ahead 20 to 30 paces and then turn right, as waymarked, at a crossroad of green tracks.

↻ *This is a junction with the Loop Walk to/from Yarpole.*

14   The path proceeds across the common to Whiteway Head where you enter Croft Wood by a stile next to a barred gate. Follow the forestry track ahead, ignoring turns to the left until you descend to a major junction at a small clearing.

↻ *This is a junction with the Loop Walk to/from Yarpole*

15   Go right to climb the bank up to a small gate on the edge of Yatton Common on the very edge of the ridge. Go left to walk along the perimeter fence of Croft Ambrey Hillfort. Ignore the path immediately to your left and other stiles on the left. You reach the magnificent viewpoint at the western edge of the hillfort.

↻ *This is a junction with the Loop Walk to/from Wigmore*

16   Bear left beside the bench to drop down through the outer ramparts to a junction with a green track. Turn left and walk up to a meeting of paths and a gate where the path to Croft Castle is marked. Ignore this and bear right, remaining outside the fence and along a route which offers great views as it follows the ridge to Ladyacre Plantation and Common Wood. The path becomes a major forestry track to descend to School Wood where it passes an old barn on the left before reaching a gate and lane.

17 Walk down the lane towards Lucton but within 300 metres go right, as signposted, along a short section of track which leads into a field by way of a stile next to a gate. Turn right and at the next boundary cross two stiles in succession. Now head slightly left through a pasture to cross another stile and ahead in a similar direction to the boundary of Pokeshouse Wood.

18 Go over the stile and prepare yourself for a sharp descent through coniferous woodland. The path is waymarked down the slope to a cross track. Go over and continue in a similar direction on a lower slope to a stile which brings you to a beautiful riverside pasture in the Lugg Valley.

19 Follow a path which runs along a semi circle of a lost meander of the river. Cross the stile in the fence and then head slightly left to a gateway. Proceed along a raised track which is presumably an old road to a gateway by a lodge. You can see Yatton Court to your left. Go through to the main A4110 road.

20 Cross the road and turn left for refreshment, accommodation and a visit to Aymestrey church or the garden centre. (The main Trail continues straight across the main road).

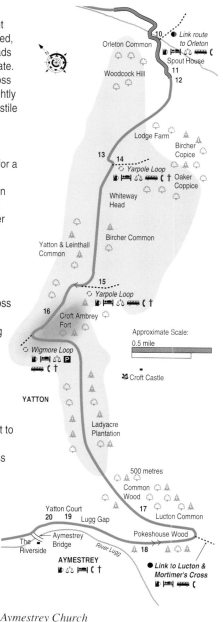

Aymestrey Church

AYMESTREY TO TITLEY

Distance: 11 miles (17 km)

Terrain

Gentle walking along a quiet road and then forest track to Lyepole Bridge. There's a strenuous climb up to the summit of Shobdon Hill Wood, 326 metres (1,069 feet) then a marvellous descent along Byton Common with spectacular birds-eye views of the valley below. There's a hard climb up to Wapley Hillfort, 325 metres (1066 feet) and then gentle walking through farmland to Titley.

Access

There is a bus service, Mondays to Saturdays, from Leominster to the turning for Covenhope where a 1.5 mile walk brings you to the Trail at Lyepole Bridge, or to Shobdon where you can join a Loop Walk which brings you to the trail at Shobdon Hill Wood. There is a limited bus service between Titley and Kington.

You will find a small amount of car parking in Titley and Shobdon, there's also a car park at Wapley.

Cut-Off Points

Lyepole Bridge, Shobdon Hill Wood (for Loop Walk to Shobdon), Byton (for Loop Walk to Shobdon) and Titley.

Refreshment

Riverside Inn and shop at Aymestrey.

Horseway Herbs tea room (half mile detour, see Ordnance Survey Pathfinder Sheet 971).

Stagg Inn, Titley.

PLACES OF INTEREST

Ballsgate and Byton Commons

Ballsgate Common lies above the hamlet and is fairly inaccessible. Byton is very steep sided and thick with bracken, bramble and scrub. Ponies are kept in the upper enclosures. You will see Combe and Byton Moor beyond Byton village, a rare survivor of marshy wetland in the County.

Shobdon Hill Wood

The ridge walk is nearly two miles long and you might come across deer and other animals, for the broadleaved woodland which borders the Mortimer Trail here is a haven for wildlife. On the Loop Walk to Shobdon is a Forest Enterprise genetics nursery where genetically improved stock are grown. Several varieties of trees are identified by label in the enclosure.

Byton

This small hamlet mainly comprising of farms is typical of deep rural Herefordshire. The trail passes near Byton's small church which is situated above an orchard and offers good views up the Lugg Valley. The church has a tympanum with an early *Agnus Dei* (Lamb and Flag) above the door.

Wapley Hill

Like Croft Ambrey, Wapley was a reasonably large hillfort with several enclosures. It covers 25 acres on this high ground. Part of the site has been cleared of trees to conserve the earthworks and this has exposed splendid views across the County. There are waymarked routes through the forest managed by Forest Enterprise.

Stansbatch

The hamlet of Stansbatch is home to a small nursery. Those wishing to divert by way of Horseway Herbs (and tea room) can do so here or at Lower Mowley. On leaving the hamlet you pass the abutments of the one time Titley Junction to Presteigne railway, a very late railway which opened in 1875 but closed to passengers in 1951 and freight in 1964.

Titley

In Norman times there was a priory in the environs of the village, an outpost of a Benedictine order from Tiron Abbey in France. It is chronicled that the roadside well by the present church was channelled from water which served the priory and some say that the waters have medicinal properties although the warning notice on the well is sufficient to ward off would be imbibers. Titley Church is mainly a Victorian restoration. Here you will find the grave of a Hungarian general, Lazar Meszarios. Having been exiled from his own country he called to visit a good friend at Eywood, a stately home near to the village. Unfortunately he succumbed to a fatal illness and was buried here. Titley Court, at the south end of the village, is an impressive building dating from the mid 19th century.

ROUTE DETAILS - AYMESTREY TO TITLEY

The Riverside Inn

22 You will see double gates on the left here and a stile. Cross it and then follow the tractor track to the edge of Sned Wood. Bear left to cross a stile at a wooden gate. The green track runs just inside the wood and bends right to run above the River Lugg. This brings you to a fishing cottage and a junction at Lyepole Bridge.

↻ *This is the junction with the Loop Walk to / from Lingen.*

23 Turn left to cross Lyepole Bridge and continue along the road until reaching a sharp left hand bend. Leave the road here, crossing the stile and head steeply up hill. After negotiating the next stile turn left and follow the forestry track. Passing a barrier bear right.

21 From the Riverside Inn turn left cross the bridge and turn next left along the road. At first you pass Aymestrey old mill to the left and then walk along the quietest of lanes in the valley of the River Lugg to Ballsgate Common, approximately one mile onward. The road bends left at Sunny Bank and then curves right to a few houses.

↻ *This is a junction with the Loop Walk to/from Wigmore.*

24 Continue to climb into the wood but as this main lane bears left keep ahead on a lesser track. This rises up the hillside and is steep in places. At the top the path eases to a summit where oak trees form an avenue. Keep ahead and soon you descend slightly to a junction.

↻ *This is a junction for the Loop Walk to/from Shobdon.*

Wapley Hill

25 Continue ahead along a wider forest track until you reach the edge of the wood and a junction. Bear right and a lesser path runs beneath a canopy of leaves down the hillside. Be vigilant for Mortimer Trail bears left to a stile. Cross this to enter Byton Common.

26 Keep to the boundary hedge on the left which runs along the top of the Common. The Common lies on a steep hillside so be sure to place your feet carefully. It descends by enclosures to the left and at a bottom corner of the lower one it bears slightly left to join another path from Shobdon.

This is a junction for the Loop Walk to/from Shobdon.

27 Turn right to descend towards the hamlet of Byton. You go through a gate to join a track which runs beneath a dwelling on your right. At the corner go up steps to cross a stile. Once in the field head slightly left to a gate. Go through it to exit onto a lane. Bear right and this little road bends left to pass by the entrance to Byton Church and then down to a junction amid working farms.

28 Go left and follow the lane to Byton Hand. There is a busy road here so take care. Turn right to pass what was the old post office and a pub. Cross here and go up the road signposted to Wapley Hill. You will not be following the road, however, for within 30 metres you go right up steps.

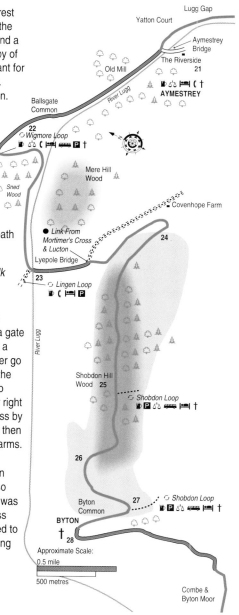

Lugg Gap

Yatton Court

Aymestrey Bridge

The Riverside **21**

Old Mill

River Lugg

AYMESTREY

Ballsgate Common

22
Wigmore Loop

Mere Hill Wood

Sned Wood

Covenhope Farm

● *Link From Mortimer's Cross & Lucton*

Lyepole Bridge

24

23
Lingen Loop

River Lugg

Shobdon Hill Wood **25**

Shobdon Loop

26

Byton Common

27
Shobdon Loop

BYTON
28

Approximate Scale:
0.5 mile

500 metres

Combe & Byton Moor

Route Details - Aymestrey to Titley - continued

29 The path uses what at one time must have been a thoroughfare of some description and is still lined with crab apple trees, the aroma of fallen fruit in autumn is delicious. The views across to Cole, Wapley and Knill hills and beyond are stunning. The path reaches a summit then dips to a stile. Cross it and go right, then drop to the next stile before heading slightly right. Cross another stile and now proceed ahead between a fence and trees.

30 On reaching a forestry track in Wapley Wood bear left. At the first junction go right and you will soon join the Forest Enterprise waymarked red route up to Wapley Hillfort through young coniferous woodland. At the track just before the ramparts of the fort turn left. At the next junction bear right and then before the house turn left. A little path cuts down to a forest track. Go left and then almost immediately right. Head slightly left to join an old avenue of trees. Descend to cross a junction with a wide forestry track and ahead to cross another.

31 At the bottom of the wood go over the stile by a gate to enter a large field. Head slightly right towards the roof tops of dwellings. Cross a stile into a narrow enclosure. Go left and walk through what appears to be the remnants of an old orchard. Cross the stile to join a road and drop right along the road into Stansbatch.

32 At the T junction go right but within 50 metres you bear left down a lane prior to the entrance to Stansbatch nursery. This delightful little lane passes a chapel and then squeezes between the abutments of a railway bridge long since gone. Pass a cottage and go over a stile by a gate to enter a lush pasture.

33 Head slightly right up the field and cross a stile. Head in a similar direction to the top far corner where you cross a stile, noting the thickness of these long standing hedges. Turn right on the road to make your way along to Mowley Farm.

Titley Well

34 Just beyond the farmhouse climb a stile on the left and then bear slightly right to a stile in the next field boundary. Keep company with the hedge on the left until it curves around to the rear of a house. Just beyond is a stile. Drop down to the road and turn right passing by a well just before reaching the B4355 road. Cross over and go left. Pass two dwellings on the right and then turn right along a track just before Titley Church (continue along the main road for refreshment at The Stagg public house).

↻ *This is a junction for the Loop Walk to/from Titley.*

35 Titley Church is to your left as the track bears slightly right to follow the hedge up the hillside. The view back across the village into the Arrow Valley is exceptional. Go through a gateway and keep ahead until the field dips right. You keep ahead to cross a stile. In the next field head slightly right to a barred gate. Once through continue ahead towards the farm but aim for a stile which is to the right of a gate. Walk ahead again to pass to the right of the farm and buildings. Cross a stile.

36 You go through a barred gate on your left and then immediately right to leave the farm by way of a high level green lane. Proceed ahead at a gate. This secluded green lane leads up to the ruins of Burnt House Farm.

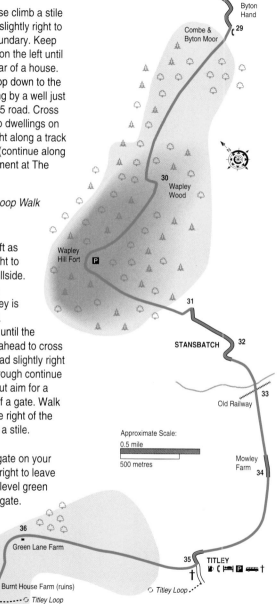

Byton Hand

Combe & Byton Moor

29

30
Wapley Wood

Wapley Hill Fort 🅿

31

STANSBATCH 32

33
Old Railway

Approximate Scale:
0.5 mile
500 metres

Mowley Farm 34

36
Green Lane Farm

Green Lane

Burnt House Farm (ruins)
⌖ Titley Loop

35 TITLEY
† ⌖ Titley Loop

TITLEY TO KINGTON

Distance: 6 miles (10km)

Terrain

Climb out of Titley to Green Lane Farm then fairly level walking along a green lane and the wooded Little Brampton Scar, 334 metres (1,095 feet) to Knill Garraway Wood. There's another ascent to Rushock Hill Common, 345 metres (1,131 feet) before descending through farmland to Kington.

Access

There is a limited bus service to Titley from Kington and Presteigne on Mondays to Saturdays. There are six buses daily (except Sundays) between Kington and Hereford where a train can be caught back to Ludlow.

There is limited car parking in Titley village but there are several car parks in Kington.

Cut-Off Point

None.

Refreshment

At Titley there is the Stagg Inn. Otherwise Kington where there are pubs, cafes and shops.

PLACES OF INTEREST

Rushock Hill Common

The Common is used for sheep rearing and offers great views across Herefordshire and into Wales. Offa's Dyke earthworks can be seen but they are much eroded here.

Kington

A traditional gap town on the banks of the infant Arrow, Kington is still very much a market and meeting place for the local farming community. The church stands at the top of the town by the earthworks of Kington Castle. In it lies the tomb of Thomas and Ellen Vaughan, who resided at Hergest Court, much associated with The Red Book of Hergest and local folklore including inspiration for Conan Doyle's "Hound of The

Kington Market Hall

Baskervilles". Hergest Croft, with exceptional gardens, parkland and a conservatory, is a ten minute walk out of town on Offa's Dyke Path.

Kington retains a traditional High Street and next to the Market Hall is the old market place where stalls are still set out. Adjacent is the town museum. Kington has justifiably gained a reputation as a walkers paradise, the Offa's Dyke Path meets the Mortimer Trail here and there is a fine network of paths around the town for those seeking shorter walks.

Bank Farm near Kington

The route of the Mortimer Trail is subject to constant upgrading and improvement. At times the route may vary from the published map and text.

Any variations in the route will be shown, at the appropriate point, by map boards and waymark signs advising walkers of the revised route.

Whilst every effort has been made to ensure the accuracy of the details given in this publication, neither the publishers nor their agents can be held responsible for any inconvenience arising from or alleged to be caused by any errors or omissions.

ROUTE DETAILS - TITLEY TO KINGTON

↻ This is the junction for the Loop Walk to/from Titley

37 Pass by the barns and go through a gate. In the pasture keep right to follow the hedge to a stile in the far corner. Cross this and go along a little path through undergrowth and two wooden gateposts onto an old road. Bear left. This brings you to a gate in approximately one quarter of a mile. Just before, turn right to cross a stile.

38 Walk along the field edge next to the wood. However, you cross a stile to enter a wood again. The path bears right away from the fencing and old scars of a quarry. It then bends left again to re-join the fencing and follows the ridge of Little Brampton Scar through mixed woodland to meet another stile. You now continue beneath a thick coniferous canopy but not for long because you soon walk between old gateposts and down steps to a forestry track. Go left and left again at the junction. Climb up to a gate where you cross a stile into a very large field. Your way is ahead.

● *This is the junction for Offa's Dyke Path. A link path strikes off right, maintaining a course mid field up to a stile and signpost on Rushock Hill where you meet Offa's Dyke Path.*

39 Mortimer Trail climbs up to a barred gate. You then follow a green track up through the gorse, maintaining a path which heads slightly left up to a remnant of the Dyke on Rushock Hill Common. Now head to the right of the clump of trees and gorse patch. Cross a stile in the next boundary then head slightly left. The path descends to the left of a gorse bank towards trees and just to the right of the dwelling, Hillgate.

40 Go over a stile by a gate to join a metalled road. This descends past the house and though a cutting to a junction. Go right but then almost immediately left to cross a stile by a gate.

41 Walk up the green track alongside a hedge. You will find a stile on the left at the top end. Go down the little dry valley to cross a stile by a gate. Then head for the left hand side of the farm buildings at Bank Farm. Go through the gate to the left of a barn and before the next gate cross a stile on the left.

42 Head slightly right across the field to the right of an oak to join a hedge. Follow this down to the corner. There's a lane leading off to the right. This is not your way. Cross into the next field. Then walk along the field edge on the left to a corner and then right to exit near the far corner.

43 Cross the B4355 Presteigne to Kington road with care. Follow the track ahead towards Mill Farm. This descends to a ford and then look for a stile on the right. Cross this and the footbridge. Proceed ahead to cross a stile in the next boundary. Continue ahead in a similar direction. The River Arrow and the old Leominster to Kington and New Radnor trackbed is to your left. Go through a gateway mid-field and at the end of the next long field cross a stile next to a gate. Go ahead to follow the hedge to a gate and stile by dwellings.

44 Follow the track ahead to the main B4355 road. Turn left and cross where appropriate. At the roundabout cross over the main A44 road to pass the entrance of the old forge. Follow the lane which bears slightly right but within a few paces go left up a narrower metalled track. This town path crosses Gravel Hill Drive and then cuts right and then left. Keep ahead now until it reaches a junction with a main path. Turn right to walk up to The Square and then left down Church Street.

● *This is a junction with Offa's Dyke Path to Chepstow (south) or Prestatyn (north)*

45 Walk down to the old Market Hall and the Burton Hotel. Go right to the Place de Marines in Kington Centre. (Tourist Information Centre nearby.)

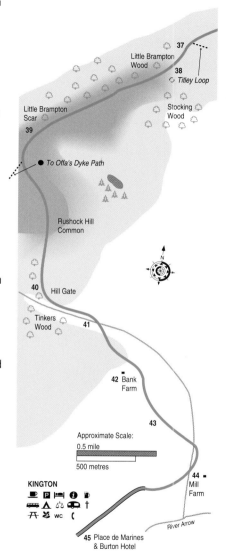

37

Little Brampton Wood

38

Titley Loop

Little Brampton Scar

39

Stocking Wood

● *To Offa's Dyke Path*

Rushock Hill Common

N

40 Hill Gate

Tinkers Wood 41

42 Bank Farm

43

Approximate Scale:
0.5 mile

500 metres

44 Mill Farm

KINGTON

River Arrow

45 Place de Marines & Burton Hotel

The Loop Walks

Yarpole Loop

Distance: 5 miles (8 km)

Terrain

Easy going with a steady climb up to Lyngham Vallet. Mainly paths and tracks with some road walking between Yarpole and Croft Castle.

Access

There is limited on-street parking in Yarpole and at Croft Castle where people are welcome to walk along established paths in the grounds or to visit the Castle when open.

Refreshment

The Bell Inn and village shop at Yarpole offer refreshment.

Places of Interest

Yarpole

The parish church, which is surrounded by a group of substantial yew trees, has an unusual detached 13th century bell tower. It stands within a central core of the village which is a conservation area with half timbered and other red brick cottage dwellings lining its main street.

Fishpool Valley is designated as a 'Site of Special Scientific Interest' reflecting the rich wildlife which has developed around the decaying fishpools.

See the main Trail for details about Croft Castle and Bircher Common - page 16.

ROUTE DETAILS - YARPOLE LOOP

● *Start at The Bell Inn in Yarpole.*

Y1 From The Bell Inn in Yarpole turn right to walk along the road to a crossroads with the B4362.

Y2 Take care here as you cross over and walk down the lane signed 'Croft Castle'. Pass Gate Lodge and the entrance to the Castle on your left and continue up the lane for another 400m/450 yards. After passing a house named 'Hillside' on your right, climb the stone steps and stile in the hedge on your left. Walk diagonally left across the field and then over a stile at the woodland edge. Walk downhill through the wood and over a footbridge. Follow the path around the left hand edge of the pool and up the bank to the Castle road.

Croft Castle

Y3 Do not join the road unless visiting Croft Castle. Instead drop down the track to the right beside the National Trust sign for Fishpool Valley. The wide path passes to the left of the pools which are currently being cleared and improved for conservation reasons. There are several paths coming in from the left but you keep ahead past the ornate stone pumphouse on the right and then further on by a small brick building on the left.

Y4 At the end of Fishpool Valley the track bends right, then left into Croft Wood. Where the track bends right, head left along the second of two paths which climbs through bracken and thorn up a gully. This reaches a forestry track at the top. Cross over to walk up a muddy track to a main forestry track. Go right into the bottom of a small clearing. Here you join the main spine of the Mortimer Trail.

Y5 Go right and follow the route ahead through Lyngham Vallet and to a stile by a gate. Once on Bircher Common, keep ahead on grazing ground until you reach a crossroads of green tracks in the far left corner. Beyond this is encroaching scrub. There's a marker post here. The main Trail peels off left to a gate and stile, but you bear right.

Y6 The green track reaches another in approximately 100 metres. Go left along it but then turn next right before the fencing of the woodland to walk between clumps of bracken.

Y7 Cross a main track which runs between Bircher Coppice on the left and Oaker Coppice to the right. There's a gate to the left here. The track continues ahead but then bears right to run along the perimeter of the wood. Ignore the straight green track leading down through the bracken on the left.

Route Details - Yarpole Loop - continued…

Y8 However, go left at the fork before a solitary oak tree. Follow this until it reaches a road at the bottom of the common by the houses. Go right to join Leys Lane.

Y9 This leads into Bircher where you walk ahead along the B4362 road to pass Bircher Hall on the right and then look for Home Farm on the right. Cross the road and a stile on the right through a camping field to cross another stile. Now head slightly right towards four trees. Go through a gateway and keep company with the hedge ahead . Cross a stile and head for the barn. Go over a stile to the right of the barn onto a metalled road.

Y10 Turn left to the junction by the handsome Pound House and go right for the short walk into Yarpole. Turn right by the stores.

Yarpole Church bell tower

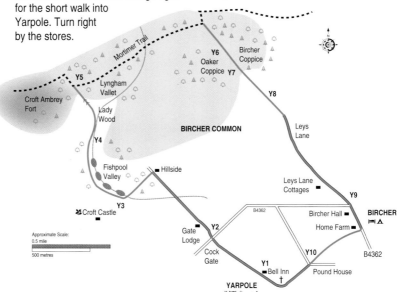

WIGMORE LOOP

Distance: 10 miles (16km)

Terrain

Steady climbs through the Wigmore Rolls but otherwise easy going with the exception of one major climb through Pokeshouse Wood and an equally steep descent from Croft Ambrey to Yatton. Return 2 mile section is along roads.

Access

There is a daily bus from Ludlow to Wigmore except Sundays. There is limited car parking in Wigmore.

Refreshment

The Compasses Hotel and Ye Olde Oak Inn in addition to the village store at Wigmore. The Riverside Inn and village store at Aymestrey.

PLACES OF INTEREST

Wigmore

Wigmore was in medieval times a significant borough in the Marches and the ruins of its extensive castle and the grand early Norman church standing on high ground evidence

Wigmore Castle

this. Both are accessible to the public. Nearby in the Vale of Wigmore stood Wigmore Priory where it is said that many of the Mortimer family are buried, the scant remains are now incorporated into Grange Farm which is private. Wigmore was the home of the Mortimer Family and affairs of state were discussed at Kings Council which were sometimes held here. Pick up the 'Welcome to Wigmore' leaflet which tells you more about the village, its history and the crafts produced hereabouts.

For details about Aymestrey and Croft Ambrey see main Trail - page 17.

Route Details - Wigmore Loop

- *Start from The Compasses Hotel, Ford Street*

W1 From The Compasses Hotel go right to walk a short distance to the main A4110 at Ye Olde Oak Inn. Go left to pass it then cross the road to walk down a bridleway just to your right. This runs up to a junction of paths. Go left up a narrow enclosed path to a stile. Cross this and go left again.

W2 This leads up to a stile and road. Go right and within 100 metres go left to cross a stile by a gate. To your left are the impressive grounds of half-timbered Wigmore Hall. Head slightly right up the valley, descending gradually to a footbridge over a brook.

W3 Once across bear right and cross a stile in fencing. Head slightly right up the bank to a barred gate situated to the right of a group of trees. Bear slightly left to cut the corner of the field and then keep company with the hedge until you reach a stile. Go over it and descend the pasture heading for the bottom far right corner while a stile exits onto a road.

W4 On the right is Barnett Wood. The road swings left and then begins to curve gently right. Go left here to cross a stile to enter a field. Keep ahead at first and you will see the stile in the next boundary near to the wood on the right. Once over keep ahead to run alongside the bottom of the bluff to a gate. Follow the track up to the farms of Lower Lye.

W5 Go left on the road and follow this down to Ballsgate Common where the main Trail joins from the right. Continue for approximately one mile to Aymestrey. Go right on the main A4110. Those seeking refreshment should bear right to The Riverside Inn and the shop.

W6 Otherwise cross the road. Go through a small enclosure to the left of the lodge then through a gate. Walk along a raised track to a gateway, then bear slightly right to cross a stile in the next boundary. The path runs in a semi circle along the edge of an abandoned meander to a stile in the fence on the left.

W7 Cross the stile and walk up the lower level of Pokeshouse Wood. This climbs up to the right to a prominent cross track. Cross the track and continue up the slope in a similar direction. The path is both steep and difficult here. It eventually reaches a stile at the top of the wood.

W8 Go slightly left across the pasture to a stile in the next boundary. Cross this and proceed in a similar direction. Cross two stiles at the next hedge and walk ahead to a stile by a gate on the left. A track leads to a road. Go left up to Lucton Common. Go through the small gate and continue ahead with an old barn to the right.

W9 This becomes a forestry track which leads through Common Wood to Ladyacre Plantation. It opens up to offer exceptional views as the track becomes a narrower greener path. Here reach a junction with a large barred gate on the right for Croft Castle. You go left along a path which skirts the lower ramparts of Croft Ambrey fort. Take the next turn right up to the viewpoint of Croft Ambrey. On a clear day you can see for miles around to the Radnorshire Forest and to Wigmore and beyond.

W10 From the viewpoint at Croft Ambrey go down a green swathe of grass through a group of windswept pine trees. Another path comes in from the left. Your path bends slightly left down the hillside but keep ahead to a cottage. Go through a gate and walk along the track to a metalled road at Yatton.

W11 Go ahead through the hamlet. As the road bends left turn right by cottages along a track which leads into fields. Go through a gateway and bear left to walk along the bottom hedge (the route has been diverted in recent years and may not be shown on your Pathfinder map). Continue with the ditch/stream on your left to reach a minor road. Turn right along this.

W12 Take care along this road because quarry lorries use it. At the junction go left and walk along a much quieter lane, passing by Leinthall Barns (accommodation). At the next junction go left for the last section into Wigmore. There's more traffic along this road.

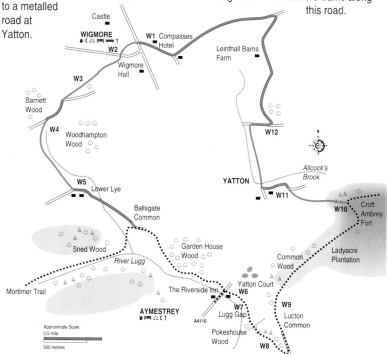

LINGEN LOOP

Distance: 5.5 miles (9km)

Terrain

The walk is mainly gentle climbs with a steep ascent at Knoll Plantation. There is a mile or more road walking between Lingen and Knoll.

Access

There is a very limited bus service. Car travellers are best to approach from Combe near to Presteigne or from Wigmore. There is limited parking near to the church or the pub.

Refreshment

The Royal George pub at Lingen.

Tea Rooms at Lingen Nursery and Gardens.

PLACES OF INTEREST

Lingen

This was at one time an influential manor held by the Lingen family and the remaining earthworks of Lingen castle can be seen behind the pretty little parish church. There is an alpine nursery in the village which is open from February to the end of October. The walk also passes the fine Georgian building of Lingen Hall which sits above the rippling waters of the Lime Brook.

Limebrook Priory

This was a nunnery established by Ralph de Lingen in the latter part of the 12th century. The 16th century cottage nearby is said to have been built with some of the remaining stones from the nunnery. Only one short section of wall remains in a field by the road.

The Lugg at Lyepole Bridge

ROUTE DETAILS - LINGEN LOOP

● *Start from The Royal George, Lingen.*

L1 From The Royal George at Lingen go left and next left by Brook House. Go through a gate and walk ahead. The path leads through the remnants of a hedge and then bends right to cross a small bridge. You then keep left to join another path which comes in from the right from Lingen Nursery.

L2 Cross a succession of footbridges which lead to a junction of green tracks. Go right and climb up to another junction of forestry tracks. Keep ahead and the track continues to rise above the valley of the Lime Brook. As the track bends slightly left go right to follow a semi-circle route along the top of the garden of Lingen Hall. Please pass with consideration. It runs along the very edge of the lawns and drops away left from the rear of the house to a junction in the wood.

L3 Go right here to descend gently closer to the Lime Brook with an old orchard to your right and a flood meadow. The path begins to bend left to rise up through woodland away from the stream, narrowed by fencing in places. It rises up to a gate.

L4 Go right to drop down to a gate to the left of a farm and an old mill. Go through the gate and bear right on the road to pass by the farm. This lane brings you to a junction by a cottage. Go left here and pass by the scant ruins of Limebrook Priory.

L5 The next section involves road walking for approximately 1 mile. You pass by the turning for Kinsham Court and rise up past houses at Bach. You then climb up to a corner where on the left is a gate which gives access to Knoll Plantation.
Caution:
Some sections of the road are very narrow. Please exercise care when walking down road sections.

L6 If you are using the loop to join the main spine of The Mortimer Trail stay on the metalled road which continues to Lye hamlet. At the junction beyond the telephone kiosk go right to Lyepole Bridge. Those coming from the main trail should follow these instructions in reverse, ie turn right at Lyepole Bridge and left at the T junction in Lye and pass by the telephone kiosk.

Otherwise go left over the gate into the plantation. The forestry track climbs steeply up to a corner. Go right and ignore turns to the left. Instead keep ahead, climbing once more, and as the track bends left go ahead on a narrow path through bracken.

L7 This approaches the boundary fence but soon curves left up to a bridle gate. Go through it and turn left to go through another gate. Walk up the green lane to a junction, with The Camp cottage seen to your right. You keep left to run along the top of the Plantation. At the far end the track bears right and you follow this for approximately half a mile towards Deerfold.

Route Details - Lingen Loop - continued...

L8 At the high level junction of roads and tracks go left along a green lane. Go through a bridle gate by a gate and continue ahead with Deepmoor Farm to your right. At the next junction go right to descend on a prominent track down towards a barn. As this bends left keep ahead down a lesser bridleway. Go through the gate and descend to a junction. Your route is ahead along a tree lined way which brings you to a cross track. Go over this and through the kissing gate. The bridleway drops down to a small bridge.

L9 Once over the bridge go left on the narrow track which becomes a metalled road. This climbs up the hillside and begins to bear right. At the corner go left over a stile by a gate. Keep ahead through the large field. You follow the remnants of a hedge and fence with New House Farm across the field to your right. Continue ahead to rise up to a gateway on the brow.

L10 Head slightly left across the next field to a stile, which cannot be seen at first, which leads into Oldcastle wood. Cross this and then follow the path which becomes a forestry track to drop down to a junction of tracks where you began the outward leg.

L11 Go right towards Lingen, and keep left as the green track bears slightly right. Cross a succession of wooden foot bridges and then keep right over a small bridge. Turn left and go through the remnants of a hedge. Keep ahead to a gate by Brook Cottage. At the road turn right.

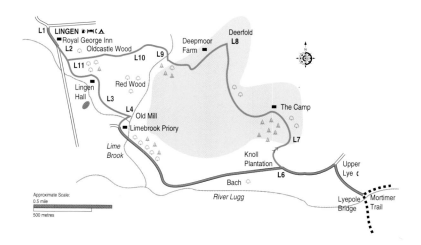

Shobdon Loop

Distance: 5.5 miles (9km)

Terrain

There is a steady ascent to Hill Barn near Byton and a ferocious climb up Byton Common to Shobdon Hill Wood. Mainly follows footpaths with some forestry tracks.

Access

Shobdon is served by buses from Leominster on Mondays to Saturdays. There is car parking in the village.

Refreshment

Shobdon has The Bateman Arms, a village store, a number of other shops and a garage.

Places of Interest

Shobdon

Shobdon church lies well away from the main village near to Shobdon Court. The existing church was built on the orders of Lord Bateman in the 1750s. He had most of the old church demolished except for the tower and the font which are still in the present church. The Romanesque style Arches were removed and can now be seen at the head of an avenue of trees. The present church is renowned for having the finest Gothic-style interior in the country.

Much of the old Court was demolished in 1933 but you can see the surviving buildings by the church including the impressive stable block.

A guide to walking in the area has been produced by Richard Morley (Parish Footpaths Officer) and is available locally.

Shobdon Arches

ROUTE DETAILS - SHOBDON LOOP

● *Start from the Bateman Arms*

S1 From the Bateman Arms go left to walk up the main road towards the Village Stores and Post Office. However, beforehand look for the old school on the right. Go up the drive immediately beyond the school to pass a cottage. This leads to a stile. Cross it and walk ahead to cross another on the left. Keep ahead to cross two more stiles.

S2 Now continue ahead with a hedge to your left on a golf course. As the hedge bends left go right across the green and then follow the opposite hedge boundary ahead to a stile. Cross this, turn left and the path runs along the edge of the field to another stile on the left. Cross this and head to the right of the house. Cross a stile into the next field and turn left. Go through the gateway and skirt a garden on the left. Cross a stile and head slightly right towards farm buildings of Downwood.

S3 Cross a stile before and turn right. Go through a gate and turn left to walk through a field above the farm. Cross a stile in the hedge and go slightly right. Cross a stile by an electric telegraph pole and head in a similar direction. A stile by a gate leads onto a road.

S4 Cross over and walk up the drive towards Belgate Farm. Cross a stile next to a gate and continue the steady climb up the hillside. At the junction of tracks go left. This passes to the left of the main farm but passes outbuildings. It bends left to two barred gates of which you go through the one on the right. Keep ahead to climb up to a junction with a path from Uphampton Farm.

S5 Keep ahead to go through a gateway into an adjacent field where there are fine views across to Hay Bluff and Merbach Hill. Go through another gateway and head slightly right to a stile which leads into a wood. The path drops down to a stile. Once over climb the hillside up to a large barn.

S6 Cross a stile on the right and through a small enclosure by Hill Barn to cross another stile near to a decaying cottage to your left. Walk ahead along the field's edge to a stile by a gate. Cross this into Byton Common. Walk a few steps down to a junction.

S7 Go right here to join the main spine of Mortimer Trail. The path bears slightly left at first but then right to climb alongside two enclosures and then ahead along the upper boundary. The common offers a magnificent birds-eye view of the hamlet of Byton as well as panoramic views to the Wigmore Rolls on the right and Radnorshire Forest on the left.

S8 Cross the stile at the very top corner. Go ahead into Shobdon Hill Wood and then bear right up a narrow path to a junction of forestry tracks. Go left here to walk almost to the summit, approximately one quarter of a mile, but at a main junction go right.

S9 The track descends to cross a diamond shaped enclosure where it meets other tracks. Keep ahead to the southern boundary where you turn left to enter the Genetic Research section (also known as the Tree Improvement Area) by way of a large gate. Walk through on a metalled road and keep right. There are forestry houses to the left. Continue on the metalled road to a junction by Park Farm.

S10 Go left here to pass by Uphampton Farm and as the road bends right and then left go ahead along a track which leads along the edge of a wood. The path bends left to Shobdon Arches and then drops between an avenue of trees to a junction of roads.

S11 Continue ahead to pass by Shobdon Church on the left and then Shobdon Court. A large poultry complex stands on the right. The road gives out through magnificent gates on the main road. Go right for the Bateman Arms.

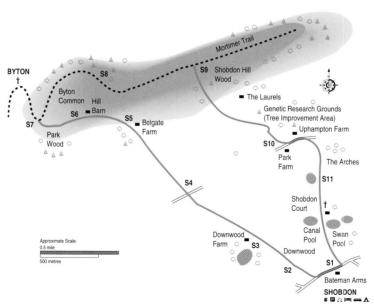

TITLEY LOOP

Distance: 3 miles (5 km)

Terrain

There is a continuous climb to Burnt House.

Access

Titley has a limited bus service from Kington. Car access by way of the B4355 between Kington and Presteigne.

Refreshment

The Stagg Inn, Titley.

Places of Interest

Titley - see detail in main route section - page 21.

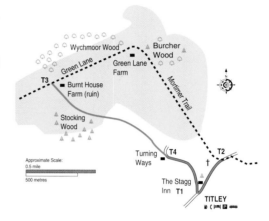

ROUTE DETAILS - TITLEY LOOP

● *Start from The Stagg Inn, Titley.*

T1 From The Stagg Inn, go left to walk down the main road to the entrance to Titley Church. Just before, to the left, is a small well erected by Lady Hastings in 1864. Before two houses go left onto Mortimer Trail (main route).

T2 Follow the section of the main route as described on pages 25 - 28 (map reference numbers 35 - 37) up to Green Lane Farm and along to Burnt House.

T3 At the ruins of Burnt House Farm go left to walk through a small wood to a stile. Cross this and follow the hedge on your left to a corner. Go left here but at the next corner cut right down to a gateway. Go through it and continue to the stile ahead. Cross it and go for the gate on the right (as there are two here). Walk ahead again to another gate. Follow the tractor track ahead to a gate and pass by a farm on the right. The lane becomes metalled at Turning Ways.

T4 At the T junction by the farm go right to descend a sunken road down to the village. Ignore the turning to the left but keep ahead to the Stagg Inn.